# The Library of Writing Skills™

# A Step-by-Step Guide to

# Descriptive Writing

Lauren Spencer

The Rosen Publishing Group, Inc., New York

*To all the amazing authors whose writings I've had the pleasure to experience. Their words have opened my eyes while making me eager for more.*

Published in 2005 by The Rosen Publishing Group, Inc.
29 East 21st Street, New York, NY 10010

**Library of Congress Cataloging-in-Publication Data**

Spencer, Lauren.
A step-by-step guide to descriptive writing /by Lauren Spencer.—1st ed.
    p. cm.—(The library of writing skills)
Includes bibliographical references and index.
ISBN 1-4042-0212-9 (library binding.)
1. English language—Composition and exercises—Juvenile literature.
2. Description (Rhetoric)—Juvenile literature. 3. Report writing—Juvenile literature.
[1. English language—Composition and exercises.]
I. Title. II. Series: The library of writing skills (New York, N.Y.)
LB1047.3.S64 2005
372.62'3—dc22
                                                        2003025769

*Manufactured in the United States of America*

# Table of Contents

# Introduction

Descriptive writing depends on details and colorful language to bring a subject to life. By describing one person, place, or thing with vivid detail, a writer can create a descriptive scene in the reader's mind. The writing becomes a snapshot of a moment because the author "zooms in" on his or her topic. He or she describes it using specific information. These details communicate to the reader's five senses, so that sight, sound, smell, touch, and taste are part of his or her experience.

Descriptive writing is used in essays, reports, fiction, nonfiction, and poetry. An author who is writing in a descriptive way climbs inside a topic and shows readers what's going on, rather than simply telling them. Although this is a technique that is often used in creative writing, it's important to learn how to write more descriptively when approaching any type of writing.

In the pages that follow, you'll find helpful examples that illustrate how to make your writing work for you by showing more and telling less. This information will help you get your descriptive piece on track as we examine ways to choose topics, gather information, and organize material. You'll also encounter examples of how adverbs, adjectives, similes, metaphors, hyperbole, and personification work to add style to descriptive writing. The importance of working with others on a final draft and options for sharing your finished piece will also be explored. Enjoy this opportunity to investigate the writer in you by using descriptive flair!

# Prewriting

The point of descriptive writing is to incorporate as much detail as possible from a single subject. Whether your subject is a person, place, or thing, the choice of a topic is a crucial one. If you've been assigned a subject already, then you've got a head start. Even so, you will still need to make the topic your own by deciding how you should direct your focus. If you haven't been given a topic, then you have many options to consider.

Ideas for descriptive writing pieces are everywhere. Keep your mind open so that you can add them to your list of potential topics. Think of a subject that is rich in sights and sounds. Notice interesting places around you. Look for ideas in the things that you read and see. At this point in the prewriting (brainstorming) process, any ideas that you have are worthy of your attention. Keep track of them. Make a list of your ideas, either written on paper, typed in a computer file, or recorded on a tape recorder.

## KEY

✔ **Think of subjects that are rich in detail.**

✔ **Choose one idea and then decide if it excites the five senses (sight, sound, smell, taste, and touch).**

✔ **Think about personal experiences related to your subject.**

✔ **Organize your information for easy usage.**

Review your list and then decide whether you will be focusing on a person, a place, or a thing. Next, pinpoint a specific subject, and take about five minutes to do some freewriting associated with that topic. You can call up moments from memory or draw from information read in books or magazines. Even a conversation that you've overheard could give you an idea. Don't stop writing. Just let your ideas flow freely during the five-minute period. Maybe the topic at the head of your page is "Places to Go in the Summertime," followed by a list of general ideas along the lines of "amusement park," "beach," and "ball games."

This is an excellent start. Now it's time to choose the best idea from the list. Remember that the main idea of your writing will be the heartbeat of your story. Everything will revolve around it. Which subject do you think is bursting with sights, sounds, and smells? Out of all of your ideas, one will likely stand out above all the others. Don't let the voice in your head say, "I can't decide." If you are having trouble making a decision, ask your friends or family to help you choose. Talk with them about all the possibilities for each of the subjects. Also, keep in mind that you can come back to this list and write other descriptive pieces later.

If you chose "amusement park" from your list, then now is the time to zoom in even closer on that topic in order to bring out the details you'll write about later.

# Getting Closer

One way to examine any subject is by thinking about things related to it. For this example, think of all of the things available at an amusement park and then group this information onto a web cluster. Write the words "amusement park" and put them in a circle in the middle of the page (see example). This is your nucleus word. All of the other words in the cluster should relate to this word. Next, make lines coming from the center circle and draw more circles at the end of each of those lines. Inside those circles, write general words about amusement parks, such as "food," "rides," "games," and "people." Now you're ready to get specific!

Draw a series of lines from your last set of circles, and attach more circles at each end. Inside these spaces, write down specific words such as "hot dogs," "cotton candy," and "popcorn" coming from the food circle or "roller coaster," "haunted house," and "Ferris wheel" from the rides circle, and so on.

Depending on the length of your piece, you can either focus on just one of these final topics, or you can include all the things you've "clustered" for a longer story. Let's say you pick "roller coaster" as your main subject. Write that at the top of a blank piece of paper and stare at it for a minute. Do you want to write about a specific memory of riding on a roller coaster from your point of view? Or would you rather write a descriptive piece as seen through the eyes of someone else? Or maybe you'd prefer to write an essay about the history of a particular roller coaster? Follow your instincts or the instructions of your teacher, and decide on your format.

If you're writing about a moment in your past, think about things that will jog your memory, like a photo album or a journal. Then go to those

# Web Cluster

An acrostic is a poem in which a word is written down the page and then each letter forms a word or sentence. This acrostic honors adjectives, which are crucial to descriptive writing.

**A**djectives

**D**escribe

**J**ust nouns to make them

**E**xciting,

**C**olorful,

**T**errific,

**I**nsightful,

**V**ery powerful,

**E**ngaging,

**S**pectacular.

sources and write down any details that come to mind. Be very specific. Don't just write down, "roller coaster at Six Flags Great Adventure." Do write down "huge steel roller coaster at Six Flags Great Adventure," "hanging upside down," "lots of people screaming," "hot day with big puffy clouds in the sky." A list of these kinds of sensory details will be helpful as you write your first draft.

If you decide to write your draft about another topic, such as the history of a specific roller coaster, then books and the Internet will offer you information to support your subject. Using these sources will help you describe your topic effortlessly. Weave adjectives, which are powerful describing words, and other details into your writing to bring the experience of riding in a roller coaster to life. Remember, in descriptive writing, your point is not to prove facts or persuade someone, but to make the reader feel as though he or she is actually experiencing whatever you have written about firsthand. Bring the reader inside the car and let him or her take the ride.

Prewriting allows a writer to pinpoint topics, gather information, and organize ideas within the main story. You'll want to keep everything you need within easy reach, so that when you begin writing, you can easily reference your lists, diagrams, or notes.

**ASK YOURSELF**

☐ Have I focused exclusively on my subject?

☐ Have I gathered an assortment of interesting details about my subject?

☐ Is all of my information accessible to begin writing my piece?

☐ Do I have appropriate tools handy, such as a dictionary and a thesaurus?

## Adverbs

Adverbs are necessary to add "movement" to descriptive writing. They describe verbs. Here are several types of adverbs:

**Time:** Adverbs that tell when, how often, or how long.
We thought the roller coaster would *never* end.

**Place:** Adverbs that tell where a person or group is going, where they are from, or just plain where.
The rollercoast looped *backward*.

**Manner:** Adverbs that tell how something is done.
The roller coaster went *quickly*.

**Degree:** Adverbs that tell how much or how little.
The roller coaster was *incredibly* crowded.

# Synonyms

Using synonyms is an excellent way to add originality to your writing. Choosing synonyms helps you to avoid boring, overused words. Synonyms are words that have the same (or nearly the same) meaning as other words. The place to find a synonym is in a thesaurus, which is like a dictionary, but instead of giving the definition of the word, it gives other words that mean the same thing.

Here's an exercise in which you can come up with synonyms from inside your head and from a thesaurus.

- ✔ Make four columns on a blank piece of paper.
- ✔ In the first column, list ten descriptive words that have to do with your topic (for example: fun, exciting, scary, etc.).
- ✔ In the second column, think of synonyms to replace your first set of words (for example: entertaining, earth-shaking, chilling, etc.).
- ✔ In the third column, use an online thesaurus to find different synonyms for your words.
- ✔ In the fourth column, use a traditional thesaurus and find more specific synonyms.

EXAMPLE:

| My Descriptive Word | A Synonym I Thought of for My Word | A Synonym from an Online Thesaurus | A Synonym from a Traditional Thesaurus |
|---|---|---|---|
| Fun | Entertaining | Amusing | Jovial |
| Exciting | Earth-shaking | Exhilarating | Rousing |
| Scary | Chilling | Alarming | Terrifying |

**Comparative:** Adverbs that compare two things by either adding -er to the end of the word, or by adding "more" or "less."

The roller coaster was *faster* than any ride I'd ever been on.
The roller coaster came *more quickly* than any other ride in the amusement park.

**Positive:** Adverbs that don't compare.

The roller coaster travels *fast*.
The roller coaster passed *swiftly*.

**Superlative** (expressing a high degree of something): By adding the suffix "-est" or the words "most" or "least" in front of an adverb, you form a superlative adverb.

The roller coaster is *quickest* when lots of people are on it.
The roller coaster rides *most smoothly* when its wheels are greased.

Now that you are more familiar with adverbs and why and how they are used correctly, make an effort to use them in your first draft. Adverbs will help you achieve accurate descriptions in your writing. Adverbs change everyday verbs into phrases that reveal specific details. If you use frequent adverbs and adjectives in your writing, then you can more clearly and effectively tell your story.

# Writing Your First Draft

By writing descriptively, you bring your reader into the story by using as many details about the topic as you can. Your first draft (sometimes referred to as the "sloppy copy") is your opportunity to transform the information from your lists and diagrams into a story. Sometimes focusing your thoughts into a flowing paragraph can be daunting. Other times, merely deciding on a descriptive topic is enough to get your mind and pen moving. Soon you'll find yourself transforming your ideas into a first draft automatically.

Either way, you want to make sure that you have everything you'll need to begin: something to write on and with, space and time enough to let it happen, and your prewriting notes. These points are crucial because the purpose of your first draft is to get all of your ideas written down without interruption.

## KEY

✔ **Have your prewriting notes within reach.**

✔ **Work on the beginning, middle, and end of your piece.**

✔ **Use active "action" verbs, descriptive language, and the five senses to bring your topic to life.**

✔ **Add adverbs and adjectives to further describe your topic.**

✔ **Don't stop writing. Keep the flow going.**

The first draft is also the place where you will find your writer's "voice." You alone bring this individual style to the written work. You may have heard the saying, "write like you talk." In descriptive writing this is especially true because you want the reader to feel as if he or she is experiencing the events through your eyes. Think about how you speak with your friends. Maybe you have a comic style of talking that makes them laugh, or you enjoy using interesting words that make people think. Some people speak formally, as if they are standing at a podium, while others speak casually. These are personality traits that make up the author's voice. When you're writing a descriptive piece, it's important to bring your individual writing style into play. Use slang (informal words) or exclamatory remarks ("argh" or "ugh") sparingly, if at all, to punctuate a particular moment.

To learn more about how the writer's voice shapes other writing, read a variety of authors' works and examine what sets them apart. Read a range of descriptive stories, poems, and articles about a variety of topics. Think about pieces you've read that made you feel as if you were a part of the moment, maybe a mystery or an action-adventure story. Re-read certain passages that made you hold your breath or had you aching to find out what happened next. Think about how the author held your interest. Chances are, the writer used some specific techniques to bring his or her story to life. Maybe he or she extended the timing of an event in order to add suspense to the story or created a mood by using certain adjectives. Attention to these kind of details sets a tone that keeps readers engaged. By paying close attention to detail and taking the time to tell your story without rushing, you can achieve the same results.

In descriptive writing, while it is important to give the readers facts about your subject, it's equally meaningful to show them what's happening in the moment. You may write, "The roller coaster was huge." If you leave it at that, you're just telling them how it is. The person reading your piece may think, "Yeah? Prove it. I bet I've seen bigger." If you add, "It reached up into the sky and cast a shadow on everything around it," then you've invited your reader to look up with you and sense the roller coaster's power.

Sensory details are an excellent way for people to experience a story. To organize the sensory details for your piece, you can map out a chart to capture them. Write "Sights," "Sounds," "Smells," "Tastes," and "Feel/Touch" at the head of each column (see example). Fill in the chart with original details or information gathered from your research.

## AMUSEMENT PARK/ROLLER COASTER SENSORY CHART

| Sights | Sounds | Smells | Tastes | Feel/Touch |
|---|---|---|---|---|
| Massive steel structure | Screaming people | Tangy smell of sweat from people | Sweet cotton candy | Hard seats that are hot from the sun |
| All the people below look like ants | Deafeningly loud | Aroma of butter from the popcorn | Bitter taste of fear | Solid safety bar pressing against my stomach |

# Time to Write!

Now you're ready to unleash your first-draft superpowers. Once you begin writing, don't stop for anything except to get inspiration from your prewriting charts and ideas. If you've chosen to describe a situation in chronological order (beginning to end), then the natural progression will be what happens in your story from one moment to the next. Or maybe you are describing something from top to bottom or the other way around. Either way, don't stop writing and don't make any spelling or grammatical corrections. You will have plenty of time to make those improvements later. The point is to let your creative brain loose onto the page right now.

If you are writing an essay, then your first paragraph should include a topic sentence to introduce your subject. If you are writing only one paragraph, then one of your first lines needs to serve that function. The topic sentence should grab the reader's attention and describe what he or she is going to find inside.

Next, you want your audience to take a closer look. The middle section of your descriptive piece should offer details about your topic. It's your responsibility to inform the reader so he or she can easily "see" and "feel" exactly what you intended. Use the synonyms you've discovered. Consider adding a variety of adjectives and adverbs if your descriptions

## ASK YOURSELF

☐ Does my first draft stay exclusively on the topic?

☐ Have I used my prewriting material to bring my topic to life?

☐ Is there a recognizable beginning, middle, and end to my piece?

☐ Have I "shown" more than I've "told"?

seem too plain. Weave together your prewriting notes and sensory chart ideas. Find a flow that takes you from one moment to the next, but don't rush your writing.

The process of writing is like a roller coaster ride: There are many twists and turns before the ride is over. And just like on an actual roller coaster, you'll probably notice when the conclusion of your written description is near. This is your chance to share any final feelings that summarize the entire experience. Example:

> During my first time on a big, red, monstrous roller coaster, I was scared. I felt like somebody was going to pull out my heart. It was fantastic when I flipped upside down and twirled in the sky. The air smelled like salt from the ocean nearby. I heard yelling. It was so scary. I was so dizzy when I got off that I fell on the ground. After that, I went on other rides with my friends Dwayne, Darryl, and Christopher. Later, we ate pizza, popcorn, and other stuff. It was a perfect day.

Notice that almost all the senses were considered when writing this piece. (Which ones can you find missing?) This example is in the format of an observational report, meaning a story about a location where all the author's observations were written down. There is dramatic and descriptive imagery to describe the author's emotions ("I felt like somebody was going to pull out my heart"). And instead of describing how the roller

## Three-minute Warm-up: Musical Pen

This exercise is a little like the game musical chairs, but instead of your body moving, your pen is going to keep writing until the music stops. Get a piece of scrap paper and put a CD into your player. Push the "play" button on a random song. With pen and paper in hand, "climb" into the song.

**Describe what you hear in detail.** Don't just write "drums," but "booming drums that shake the room."

**Describe your emotions and how this music makes you feel.** Do you feel like running up a mountain? Surfing on a wave? Going to a party? Are you excited? Sad? Happy?

**Describe where this music takes your imagination.** Are you on a beach? Write about the scene in detail. What's going on around you? What would you be eating and drinking? What do the people look like (or are you alone)?

When the music stops, end your thoughts and finish writing.

coaster felt to the touch, the description was more about how the writer felt on the inside. By allowing your audience to glimpse how you feel emotionally, you are providing them with a way to be engaged in the writing that is personal and unique.

# Exploring Different Techniques

When writing, it's advisable to avoid the bland and boring. By using figurative language such as similes and metaphors, your readers will be further drawn into your descriptive story.

## Similes

Whenever you compare two different people, places, or things by using the words "like" or "as," you are using a figure of speech known as a simile. When making comparisons that are unexpected, as similes often are, you keep your writing lively. Similes point out the similarities of two things that wouldn't normally go together. For instance, you wouldn't compare a roller coaster to a Ferris wheel because those two things are alike, but you could compare a roller coaster to a snake.

## KEY

✔ **Understand how different figures of speech work to make writing more interesting and exciting.**

✔ **Weave these literary techniques into your first draft.**

Use your imagination to connect two unlike items and find their similarities. Think of how they both look, sound, and feel. A roller coaster and a snake are both long and curvy. They can both take your breath away with fear. Use these details along with "like" or "as" to make your comparisons. Example:

> The roller coaster is like a curvy snake. It is as exciting as a snake because it takes my breath away. The roller coaster is like a snake when it moves and hisses in my ear.

## Metaphors

The metaphor is also a figure of speech. It is similar to the simile because it also makes a comparison, but it does not use the words "like" or "as." Therefore, the roller coaster becomes the snake. Compare the metaphorical sentences below with the similes above to see how they've changed. Example:

> The roller coaster is a curvy snake. It is an exciting snake because it takes my breath away. The roller coaster is a snake when it moves and hisses in my ear.

# Hyperbole

Hyperbole is figurative language that you probably use without even realizing it. It is extreme exaggeration. With hyperbole, you take an element of truth and then stretch it. Have you ever said (or thought), "I'm so tired that I could sleep forever"? While the truth is that you may be exhausted, you probably aren't about to go to sleep until the end of time. This is an example of hyperbole.

To make your writing more expressive by using hyperbole, focus on one particular moment. Now, think of all the outrageous ways in which you can stretch the description of what you're trying to say without losing sight of your point. Example:

> The roller coaster was going so fast that
> my heart popped out of my body and fell onto
> the tracks. My teeth chattered so loudly
> that you could hear them in China. The ride
> went on forever.

# Personification

When you read the word personification, you get a clue as to what it means. Personification is when you give human characteristics to something that is not human, and hence "person" is the first half of the word. This is a great technique to use in writing because you are bringing your topic to life and making it three-dimensional.

Read through your piece and look for things that can become more lifelike. Perhaps a house or a car appears to have a "face" or a tree has big powerful "arms." Giving inanimate objects human attributes will introduce a new dimension to your descriptive writing. Example:

> The roller coaster's tunnel-like mouth swallowed everyone and then spit them out on the other side. Its hands held people in their seats while it twirled them around its massive head.

# Local Color

In descriptive writing, it is important to "paint" your topic with local color by including the surroundings common to the subject that you're writing about. Your goal is to bring the reader into the scene so he or she can fully experience the surroundings. A good way to capture these facts is to use your imagination to look around. As you imagine the vivid details of the scene, add this information to your writing. Example:

> As I stood in line waiting to get on the roller coaster, I noticed a sign that said "Twister" in red neon lights. When I looked in the other direction, I saw a tall clown making people laugh. Some teenagers were trying to get the clown's attention. His name was Bingo, and he had rainbow-colored hair, big floppy overalls, a large red nose, and huge orange shoes. He

> walked over to a food stand that sold snacks. The hot
> dogs looked like they'd been rolling on the grill
> for 100 years, while the blue and pink cotton candy
> appeared to be melting in the sun. At the game
> booths, a young guy was yelling out to the clown
> for him to come over.

# A Little Goes a Long Way

You might be wondering about where and how often these figures of speech might be best employed. Find places in your writing where they can enhance its detail. Don't go overboard by trying to squeeze a metaphor or simile in every sentence. If you overuse figurative language, your writing will sound artificial.

|  | Simile | Metaphor | Hyperbole | Personification |
|---|---|---|---|---|
| **Roller coaster** | Looked like a snake. | Is a snake. | So fast that my heart popped out of my body. | Massive head and tunnel-like mouth ate everyone up. |
| **Food stand** | The cotton candy looked like blue and pink clouds. | The cotton candy was a blue and pink cloud floating on top of a white stick. | The hot dogs looked like they'd been rolling on the grill for 100 years. | |

## Writing with Style

Pick one of the following situations and write about it using figures of speech such as similes and metaphors. Try other devices, too, such as hyperbole and personification.

- You are walking home from a friend's house after dark and you take a shortcut through a graveyard. Describe the experience.

- It's the day after the last day of class. Describe your classroom.

- After being led astray during a field trip, you get locked in a museum all night. Describe how you spent your time.

To locate specific places where figurative language would improve your writing, it is helpful to create a chart (see example). Take a piece of paper and write the techniques along the top line. Then, using your draft, make a list of places down the left-hand margin where you think your writing could be improved by adding more detailed information. When used effectively, figurative language can enliven a written work like nothing else can. Once you familiarize yourself with these techniques, you'll find that you'll include them in your writing naturally.

### ASK YOURSELF

- ☐ Have I found several places in my piece to include specific figures of speech?

- ☐ Are these places where I am enhancing the flow and style of my writing?

# Revising Your First Draft

The word "revise" means "to go back and survey." It is the act of revisiting your writing to improve its detail and sentence structure. This process will give you a chance to polish your piece until it shines. Start your revision with a clean slate—whether that is a fresh piece of paper or a blank computer screen—along with all of the related writing you've done so far and your detailed lists and charts.

Carefully read over your first draft and take note of how the writing flows. This rhythm takes the reader from point to point while holding his or her interest from the beginning of the piece to its end. Story and sentence structure work to achieve this progression by making sure that subjects maintain clarity and order. Check that your sentences follow one another smoothly, whether chronologically or by

## KEY

✔ **Focus on clear transitions between sentences and paragraphs.**

✔ **Make sure that your sentence structure is varied.**

✔ **Expand your details so that they are as rich and sensory driven as they can be.**

✔ **Check that literary techniques and descriptive words are used effectively and not overused.**

using a less obvious format. Variety in your writing will help avoid boredom through repetition.

# Transitions

Transitions are the words and phrases used at the beginning of sentences and paragraphs to connect one idea to another. They help keep readers on track and lead them from one thought to another without confusion. Don't depend on just one transition to get you from sentence to sentence, for instance:

> *Then* I got on the Ferris wheel. *Then* it started to move. *Then* I screamed.

Using the same transition for every sentence in a paragraph will bore any reader. By using different transitions, excited readers will be swept along into the piece. Be creative.

- Start a sentence with an adjective that gives readers details about your topic.

- Begin a sentence by determining specific information from your sensory chart.

- Try starting a sentence with a phrase that tells when something took place.

- Introduce your piece by describing where you are.

- Begin with a phrase that explains something specific about your subject.

# Compound Sentences

When two sentences (also known as independent clauses because they can stand on their own) merge, they make a compound sentence. You can join like-minded sentences together by using punctuation, like a semicolon.

**The bumper cars were fun; people were screaming their heads off.**

Or a conjunction—words like "and," "or," and "but" can be deployed.

**The bumper cars were fun, and people were screaming their heads off.**

# Complex Sentences

When you have a statement (a clause) that is not a complete sentence, it is known as a dependent clause because it needs another sentence to make it whole. A complex sentence contains an independent clause (complete sentence), along with one or more dependent clauses.

Dependent clauses can begin with a relative pronoun like "who," "that," or "which."

**The clown, who was incredibly tall, made people laugh until they cried.**

The sentence could have stood alone as:

**The clown made people laugh until they cried.**

But adding the phrase "who was incredibly tall" gives it more detail.

| When describing a detail to do with time | Explaining the cause and effect in in a situation | Showing the relationship between two conditions |
| --- | --- | --- |
| after | because | although |
| before | since | while |
| as soon as | if | so that |
| until | even though | in order that |
| when | unless | provided that |

A complex sentence can also employ a subordinate conjunction to bring together independent and dependent clauses.

**Because the day was sunny, the amusement park was packed with people.**

In this case, the word "because" sets up cause and effect. Due to the weather, people came to the amusement park. Here are some examples of common subordinating conjunctions. They are always used at the beginning of a dependent clause.

## Zoom In

In order to add even more detail to your writing, look for places where you can examine a moment further. Think about how each sentence is like a snapshot where you can zoom in for a closer view. If you

**ASK YOURSELF**

☐ Were elements added to my story to make it richer in content?

☐ Does it flow from one moment to the next smoothly?

☐ Is it ready to share for a final edit?

are writing about someone's clothing, describe the color, but then find a smaller detail to focus on, like a button. Get inside of that button and describe the thread used to fasten it. Through your specific descriptions, your readers will have the ability to "experience" your topic. Example:

## Mr. Bumper Car

Mr. Phelps is responsible for the bumper car ride at River Run Amusement Park. He has worked at the park for thirty-five years. I don't know how old he was when he started because while I was talking to him last week, he refused to tell me his age.

*sensory details* → All day he is surrounded by screaming kids, the smell of burning rubber from the wheels of the cars on the tracks, and the endlessly blinking lights. Mr. Phelps told me that he sometimes ← *hyperbole* thinks of the cars as living things, since they wink at people when their headlights go on and off.

*personification* → As I talked to Mr. Phelps, who is as tall as a tree with skin like leather from being out in the *simile* → sun, I noticed how his hands were constantly moving the levers. They control the blinking lights and loud music that plays during the ride. His dark brown hands wrapped around the controls tightly. I noticed how dirty his nails were and that he wore a gold ring on his pinky finger. The ring had a little diamond in it that would catch the light every once in a while. When he took his hands away from the controls, they shook a little bit. It seemed as if Mr. Phelps had worked at the bumper car ride forever. ← hyperbole

He pointed out a boy with dark hair in one of the cars and told me that this teenager had visited the ride every day for the last two weeks, always asking for the same blue and silver car. When I → descriptive detail looked at this particular customer, I saw that he was laughing and waving his arms around as if he'd never had that much fun in his entire life. Both Mr. Phelps and I thought that was entertaining.

hyperbole

In the essay above, the writer used figurative language to bring this non-fiction descriptive piece to life. Its use of simile, hyperbole, and personification also adds rich details. One moment where the writer added depth was the passage about Mr. Phelps's hands. Note how the writer described Mr. Phelps's dirty nails and his shiny pinky ring. Varied transitions and sentence structure also worked to make the piece flow.

Now that you have read this detailed and descriptive passage, return to you own draft and examine it for places where you can add specific details. Think of ways to describe people, places, or events by using metaphors or similes, hyperbole, and personification. Although might not end up using everything that you've thought of in your draft, thinking of your writing in this way will help you develop a distinctive author's voice.

# 5

# Proofreading and Editing

You are now ready to finalize your descriptive piece through the process of proofreading and editing. Proofreading is a method of going over your writing from beginning to end and checking it for spelling, grammar, and content problems. If you are proofreading your work on paper, it is helpful to use a different-colored pen to make changes.

Begin by examining your draft for spelling errors. If you are working on a computer, engage the spell-check function and change mistakes as needed. If you are working on a hard copy (written out in longhand), circle any words in question and then write in the correct spellings after looking them up in the dictionary.

Along with spelling, focus on the content of your sentences. When writing descriptively, you want the reader to feel involved. Writers use engaging and complete descriptions

## KEY

✔ **Polish your piece by checking spelling, punctuation, capitalization, word usage, and grammar.**

✔ **Work with a partner or teacher to ensure that your writing is the best that it can be.**

✔ **Add a title that engages the reader.**

to interest their readers. Just as it's frustrating when someone tells a story and then trails off without filling in important details, the same is true in writing. If you have incomplete sentences or ones that do not contain a subject and a predicate, now is the time to fix them. Examples:

**Subject:** The focus of the sentence.
**Predicate:** The part of the sentence that describes the subject.
**The roller coaster (subject) is massive (predicate).**

A simple predicate is a single verb.
**The roller coaster (subject) moves (predicate).**

Check that your verb tenses are correct throughout your writing. Are you writing about something that's already happened? Then your verbs need to reflect the past tense. Is it happening now? Then employ the present tense. If you are writing about something that hasn't happened yet, then the future tense comes into play. Examples:

**I *went* on the water ride. (Past)**
**I *am going* on the water ride. (Present)**
**I *will go* on the water ride. (Future)**

Examine your writing to make sure that your sentences agree. This is like making sure you're wearing socks that match. If you are using a singular subject, then a singular verb goes along with it. If you have more than one subject, then a plural verb goes with those subjects. Examples:

The room *is* massive. (singular)
The people *were* dancing. (plural)

Once you've made corrections throughout your piece, use a proof-reading checklist to review your work. If you answer "no" to any of the following questions, then take some time to go over the entire draft again.

- Are all words spelled correctly?
- Are all sentences complete thoughts with both a subject and predicate?
- Do all verb tenses agree?
- Do all sentences begin with a capital letter and end with a period, question mark, or exclamation point?
- Do all proper nouns start with a capital letter?
- Do all nouns agree with their verbs?

# Choosing a Title

Your title is the first thing that catches the reader's attention and introduces him or her to your work. Think of all the times that you may have ignored a movie based on its title. Now, apply that same sort of evaluation to titles that you're considering. You want to create a title that quickly captures a person's interest and makes him or her curious. While you may have been using a first-draft ("working") title, now is the time to refine it into something that grabs the reader. During the process of revising, title ideas may pop into your head. Write them down so that you have plenty of choices when it comes time to commit. It's also a good idea to wait until your revisions are finished in order to decide on a final title. Waiting will give you the latitude to review your finished version to see what stands out. Writers occasionally get trapped into writing their story based on what their title suggests, thereby losing the freedom to see where the story may take them.

Another way to choose a title is to locate a specific detail and then try to create a title around that fact. Other types of titles that may spark a reader's interest might be in the form of a question. Seek advice from a teacher, classmate, or friend if you are still unable to decide on an appropriate title for your piece.

Sharing your work is an important way to find out how engaging your descriptive story is. Reading your work aloud can help with punctuation questions, subject clarity, and overall content. Sometimes individuals can become so involved in their own writing that they need to get someone else's opinion. This is a good opportunity to hear feedback on what does and doesn't work in your writing.

When you partner with someone, decide whether you are going to read and take notes on each other's work silently or whether you are going to read aloud to each other while making notes for discussion. Another excellent way to

**ASK YOURSELF**

- [ ] Will the reader's attention be grabbed by my title?

- [ ] Have I addressed all the issues brought up in my partnering?

- [ ] Have I rewritten the piece to reflect all of my corrections?

obtain feedback about your writing is to read it out loud to a group. Once you've read it through, encourage the audience to ask about confusing words or unclear sentences. Keep track of these items by making notes on your page next to where the question appeared. Example:

## Who's at the Door?

Nicole went into the empty house alone. She was going to go with Millie, her best friend, but when everyone started making fun of her, she quickly changed her mind and announced that she'd go by herself. It was late in the afternoon and getting dark already, since the summer was ending. The day had been a fun one filled with fast rides and lots of greasy food, but the house on the walk home was as exciting as everything else they had done today.

As soon as Nicole entered the front door of the dank-smelling house, she began to have second thoughts. Although she had just turned thirteen, sometimes she felt like a little kid. She had decided that she would show her friends how brave she was by going through the entire house on her own. It smelled like dirty socks, and as she felt her way around the rooms, her hand touched something sticky and warm. She just barely stopped herself from screaming and had to take deep breaths to keep from running out of the room.

## Proofreading Symbols

If you receive your piece back from someone who has proofread it, there may be odd-looking marks on the page. These are called proofreading symbols.

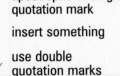 insert a comma

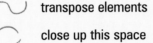 delete

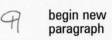 a space needed here

apostrophe or single quotation mark

transpose elements

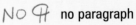 begin new paragraph

insert something

close up this space

NO ⌐ no paragraph

use double quotation marks

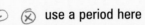 use a period here

> Nicole looked around, but could only see darkness.
> It did seem like the walls were breathing, though,
> and her heart was pounding so loudly that it felt
> like it was going to explode. She heard a loud
> rattle behind her and wondered if more people had
> come inside. Suddenly the door blew open with a
> loud bang. Something flew right toward her. The
> last thing she remembered before fainting was,
> "What is it?"

A question was used for the title of this descriptive piece, which poses a mystery and ties into the topic of the story. The subject itself is described through the eyes of the main character using the five senses, hyperbole, personification, and simile. Complex and compound sentences were used to vary the structure of the writing, while transitions maintained a smooth flow.

# Presentation

Now that you have edited and polished your written work, there are a few final things that you can do to improve it. These decisions about your work have to do with its overall presentation to others.

People are frequently drawn to things that are pleasing to the eye. It's no different when it comes to presenting your writing. Presenting your piece in a nice package shows that you, the writer, have pride in your work. This shouldn't in any way be a substitute for a well-written piece, but it will go a long way in showing that you're pleased with what you've produced.

Step back and look at your writing from a reader's perspective. If you are writing your piece by hand, then neatness in both handwriting and paper stock are important. Also, be sure to use a pen that makes marks that are easy to read. If you are typing the piece on a computer, the type style and font size should enhance the reader's experience. Look for visual

## KEY

✔ **Examine your entire piece to make sure that it is visually pleasing.**

✔ **Decide if pictures or graphics will enhance your writing.**

✔ **Share it with others.**

elements to include that could enhance your story. Check with your teacher before adding artwork to make sure that this is acceptable for the assignment.

Most important, you want to make sure that anyone who enjoys your piece knows who wrote it. Feature your name in a prominent place. Traditionally, the author's line is either at the top of the piece (in the margin with your heading or after your title) or at the bottom of the piece (following the story). Taking ownership for your work is important. Lastly, to feel confident that you are indeed presenting your best work, double-check your final version.

# Presentation Checklist

- Is the handwriting or type style (including font size) clear and easy to read?

- Is the piece printed on clean paper?

- Is my name clearly visible?

- Is the title at the top visible and underlined?

- If there are graphics, are they clear and arranged on the page in an interesting way?

# Beyond the Classroom

There are many ways in which you can share your writing. Since descriptive writing focuses on involving the reader in a moment, holding a reading of the work can be fun. This is something that professional writers sometimes do in order to present their work to the public. Readings are often held in bookstores or libraries, but you can put one together anywhere. Here are some suggestions:

Find a comfortable spot to hold the reading. This can be your house, the park, or any space that doesn't have too much noise or traffic.

Tell the people you've invited what the topic of your piece is and ask them to bring similar contributions to share, whether stories about their own experiences or other related writing. Let them know that each person will have a certain amount of time to read.

Print up invitations that include a line from your piece that can be a "preview" to make people curious. This is a little like what film studios do to get you to see their movies. Example:

| Look at Me |
| :---: |
| I rise into the sky |
| Over the baby blue water. |
| I am made of metal with hard chairs |
| and soft seatbelts that cradle screaming people. |
| When I move, I go fast, like a projectile. |
| I let people taste the blowing wind. It is warm. |
| The air smells like salt. |
| I am the roller coaster at Coney Island. |

This descriptive poem relies on the senses, a simile, and personification to deliver its point and take the reader on a ride.

## Listening In

In order to get the most out of the moments when authors present their work, try these "active" listening tips:

- Look at the speaker when he or she is reading.

- Do not interrupt or cause distractions.

- Pay attention to the speaker's tone of voice. This will let you know how strongly he or she feels toward his or her subject.

- When the reading is over, clap to show your appreciation.

Poems can be fun to write and send to friends who can add to them and circulate them like a chain letter. Eventually, the poem comes back, and you can read how it evolved.

Writing descriptively can be fun and rewarding. By learning to employ the writing techniques we have learned in this book, any type of writing can be vastly improved upon. Remember to ask yourself what you would want to learn about your subject. If you deliver these details and more, you can be certain that all of your future writing assignments will shine.

**ASK YOURSELF**

- Would I be proud to show my descriptive piece to others?

- What would I do differently and/or the same next time?

- What is the most interesting thing I learned about myself while writing this piece?

# Glossary

**adjective** A word that describes nouns or pronouns.

**adverb** A word that describes verbs, adjectives, and other adverbs.

**brainstorming** Collecting ideas by talking openly and writing down all the possibilities; freewriting.

**chronological** Being in the order of occurrence.

**complex sentence** A sentence formed by one independent clause and one or more dependent clauses.

**compound sentence** A sentence in which two independent clauses are joined together with a coordinate conjunction.

**conjunction** A word used to connect individual words or groups of words.

**constructive criticism** Helpful remarks given about shared writing.

**content** The substance of a piece; what is contained in a body of writing.

**dependent clause** A clause that cannot stand on its own and depends on the rest of a sentence to make sense.

**essay** A piece of writing in which a single topic is presented, explained, and described in an interesting way.

**feedback** The response of the reader or audience to a piece of writing.

**fiction** Literature that is created from ideas designed by the author and not based on facts.

**figurative language** Language used to create a special effect; words and phrases that usually do not mean what they appear to mean such as hyperbole or personification.

**figure of speech** A device such as a metaphor or simile that is used by writers to create a special meaning.

**first draft** The first version of a piece.

**format** The style or manner of a piece of writing.

**freewriting** The process of exploring thoughts, feelings, and ideas by writing them down in any order that comes to mind.

**grammar** The guidelines and rules followed in order to speak and write acceptably.

**hyperbole** Figurative language that uses extreme exaggeration in order to emphasize a point.

**independent clause** A clause that expresses a complete thought and can stand alone as a sentence.

**margin** The edge, border, or plain space around a page.

**metaphor** A figure of speech that compares two different things without using "like" or "as."

**nonfiction** A piece of writing that is factual.

**paragraph** A passage of writing usually made up of several sentences about one topic.

**personification** Figurative language in which a nonhuman thing is given human characteristics.

**phrase** A group of related words that does not express a complete thought.

**predicate** The part of the sentence that says something about the subject.

**proofreading** Checking the final copy for any errors.

**punctuation** Marks used in writing to support the piece.

**report** An account given or opinion expressed about a particular topic.

**revise** To go back and survey.

**sensory details** Details that use the five senses to describe something.

**simile** A figure of speech that compares two different things using "like" or "as."

**"sloppy copy"** The first draft.

**subject** The topic of a writing piece.

**superlative** A type of adverb or adjective that indicates the highest degree.

**synonym** A word that has the same meaning as another word.

**thesaurus** A book similar to a dictionary, except that it offers synonyms instead of word definitions.

**title** The name of a piece of writing.

**topic** The subject of a piece of writing.

**topic sentence** A sentence that describes what the piece of writing is about.

**transition** A phrase that ties two ideas together smoothly.

**verb** A word that shows action or links the subject to another word in the sentence.

# For More Information

*Teen Ink*
P.O. Box 30
Newton, MA 02461
e-mail: editor@teenink.com
Web site: http://www.teenink.com

When Teens Write
P.O. Box 356058
Briarwood, NY 11435
Web site: http://www.teenwriters.net

## Web Sites

Due to the changing nature of Internet links, the Rosen Publishing Group, Inc., has developed an online list of Web sites related to the subject of this book. This site is updated regularly. Please use this link to access the list:

http://www.rosenlinks.com/lws/desc

# Getting Published

*Merlyn's Pen*
Fiction, Essays, and Poems by
   America's Teens
P.O. Box 910
East Greenwich, RI 02818
e-mail: merlyn@merlynspen.com
Web site: http://www.merlynspen.com

*Skipping Stones*
Multicultural Children's Magazine
P.O. Box 3939
Eugene, OR 97403
e-mail: editor@skippingstones.org
Web site: http://www.
skippingstones.org

*Stone Soup*
A Magazine by Young Writers
   and Artists
P.O. Box 83
Santa Cruz, CA 95063
Web site: http://www.stonesoup.com

*Teen Ink*
P.O. Box 30
Newton, MA 02461
e-mail: submit@teenink.com
Web site: http://www.teenink.com

*Teen Voices*
P.O. Box 120-027
Boston, MA 02112
e-mail: womenexp@teenvoices.com
Web site: http://www.teenvoices.com

*Young Voices Magazine*
P.O. Box 2321
Olympia, WA 98507
e-mail: support@
   youngvoicesmagazine.com
Web site: http://www.
   youngvoicesmagazine.com

# For Further Reading

Culham, Ruth. *6 + 1 Traits of Writing: The Complete Guide*. New York: Scholastic, 2003.

Kemper, Dave, Verne Meyer, and Patrick Sebranek. *All Write: A Student Handbook for Writing and Learning*. Wilmington, MA: Great Source Education Group, 2001.

Mandelbaum, Paul, ed. *First Words: Earliest Writing from Favorite Contemporary Authors*. Chapel Hill, NC: Algonquin Books, 2000.

Meyer, Stephanie, and John Meyer, eds. *Teen Ink: Our Voices, Our Visions*. Deerfield Beach, FL: HCI Teens, 2000.

Sunley, Laura. *Fun with Grammar: 75 Quick Activities & Games That Help Kids Learn About Nouns, Verbs, Adjectives, Adverbs, and More*. New York: Scholastic, 2002.

# Bibliography

Ace Writing. "The Writing Process." 2002. Retrieved July 7, 2003 (http:// www.geocities.com/ fifth_grade_tpes/index.html).

Armstrong, Tricia. *Information Transformation*. Markham, ON: Pembroke Publishers, 2000.

Creative Writing for Teens. "How to Format a Manuscript for Publication." 2003. Retrieved June 20, 2003 (http://www.teenwriting.about.com/cs/formatting/ht/FormatManu.htm).

Creative Writing for Teens. "Tips on Writing from the Creative Writing for Teens Community." 2003. Retrieved August 26, 2003 (http://www.teenwriting.about.com/library/submissions/bltipssub.htm).

English Biz. "Writing to Describe and Original Writing." 2003. Retrieved October 16, 2003 (http://www.englishbiz.co.uk/mainguides/describe.htm).

Feder, Barnaby J. "With the Apples Arriving by E-Mail, Teachers Adapt." *New York Times*, August 14, 2003, p. G5.

Guernsey, Lisa. "A Young Writer's Roundtable, via the Web." *New York Times*, August 14, 2003, p. G1.

"Guide to Grammar and Writing." 2003. Retrieved August 1, 2003 (http://webster.commnet.edu/grammar/index.htm).

Hewitt, John. "Fifteen Craft Exercises for Writers." Writers Resource Center Online. Retrieved June 25, 2003 (http://www.poewar.com/articles/15_exercises.htm).

Kemper, Dave; Patrick Sebranek; and Verne Meyer. *All Write: A Student Handbook for Writing & Learning*. Wilmington, MA: Great Source Education Group, 1997.

Literacy Education Online. "The Write Place Catalogue." 1997. Retrieved July 10, 2003 (http://leo.stcloudstate.edu/acadwrite/descriptive.html).

Scholastic for Teachers. "Writing With Writers." 2003. Retrieved June 20, 2003 (http://teacher.scholastic.com/writewit).

Stone Soup. "Links for Young Writers." 2004. Retrieved June 20, 2003 (http://www.stonesoup.com/main2/links.html).

Teacher Created Materials. "Language Arts." 2000. Retrieved July 21, 2003 (http:// www.teachercreated.com).

# Index

## About the Author

Lauren Spencer is originally from California and now lives in New York City, where she teaches writing workshops in the public schools. She also writes lifestyle and music articles for magazines.

## Credits

**Designer:** Geri Fletcher; **Editor:** Joann Jovinelly